READING THE GROUND

Reading the Ground

poems by

TERA VALE RAGAN

HILARY THAM CAPITAL COLLECTION

2014 Selections by Jeanne Larsen

THE WORD WORKS

WASHINGTON, D.C.

Cover art: Lorna Alkana, "Tera Reads the Ground," 2013.
Author photograph: Mara Jamé Ragan
Book design: Susan Pearce Design
Library of Congress Control Number: 2013916645
International Standard Book Number: 978-0-915380-91-6

Gratitude to publications in which poems have appeared, some in
earlier versions:

16th & Mission Review: "The Orchard."
Barely South Review: "Exiled."
Ekleksographia: "The Painter on the Charles Bridge,"
    "Torch No. 1," and "Below the Tatra Mountains."
Hot Metal Bridge: "There was a seed planted…" and
    "The Monday Garbage Man."
Rattle: "Sunday Picnic on the Vltava River."
Transfer Magazine: "Big Bertha of the Steel Mills."

Special thanks to Erick Macek for assistance with proofreading
the Slovak.

For my parents, James and Debora,
without whom much of this family history
would have remained unknown.

Thank you for giving me the world,
and with it, the inspiration for these poems—
a strength of family that now lives on within these pages.

CONTENTS

1 Betrothal

When asked what she thought of him when they first met

she said that there was something about him. How he seemed
to take up all the room in the air, a bit sure of himself.
She had thirteen children with him.

A Hill Between

Cernina and Turcovce, Slovakia

Footprints and cattle hooves carve a path up and over the large mass sloping green between the two villages, the hues of patched earth, and past the bundled white hay gathered across the separate flats of green wilder. Alongside the path, the thorn grass is still high enough to get down deep into it. Clover and mushroom patches speckle the spots of grass shaded from the aspen growing tall along the western slope. On a clear blue day, the further I walk up, I can see the highest peak of the volcanic range, the silent Vihorlat, waiting to erupt its secrets from the east. In August, like this one, the wild flowers bloom to a sea of dandelion and sunflowers boughing up their necks to the threshed sky. I imagine him, my grandfather, walking this way, leaving Turcovce as the sun rises, picking goldenrods as he climbs upward and reaches into his pocket for the silk handkerchief. After meeting her twice before, today he'll throw it at her feet. He tastes the green wings of the dandelions and runs his fingers through the tall blades of grass like I do. When we reach the top we breathe in the wet air, take in the scent of pine and know we are one with the sky. This is the path he follows downhill to Cernina. This is the hill he crosses to see her. This is the border that did not separate them.

The Proposal

On their first meeting she knew:
he was sturdy earth, the thickbark
pine, the smoke on the hillside.

On their second, he knew:
sixteen years and ocean wide, the blue
of her eyes could control waves.

On the third, gulls sang gossip into
that muteair morning as if they knew:
she was his force of gravity.

Engulfing him in high tide,
she tipped his anchorset heart over—
He tossed   a
            silkkerchief
                              at
                                   her
                                        pooling
                                          feet.

The Bridal Dance

Spinfeet and heels
  dig a *czardas* [1]
      into the danceboards.
By midnight
the room is topsy
with *Slivovitz* [2]
  and breath.

The hemsilk of her dress
     swishes
wedding wreathes around the room.

Tipsy, his heated hands throw coins
             down
         to wetwood,
a failed suitor
    dreaming of sweat
       beneath
her garterlace.

In less than a
    stabsecond
a silver splinter
   of steel,

the ice pick,
an eye pick
   in his hand,
     shaves
       through
      the
      iris—

a brother,
his straw-thin body at her feet.

Bloodlace takes color against
her ankles.

Eyes for an Eye (*Oči pre oko*) [3]

Legs thrash
through Cernina hills,

                quick air,

          tall grass.

      Twigs are bent

        compasses

for direction.

He is wanted:

      Oči pre oko.

      They track him.

          Smoke through

            the trees,

a wooden *chata*

         cradled

      by bramble thorn,

        rabbit brush.

At first,

      a flash

of fists—

      his body held down,

briars

at his eyes—

      splatterings of red and black.

      Oči pre oko,

         light rubbed out,

          like fire stubbed

        to ash.

The heat of red now wet on his face,
    black air
            bleeding into
       darkness.

He is left breathing,
reading splinters in the floorboards.

II Incarceration

On a common walk before dinner through the hills

and back to the house, his uncle points out across the village towards a small block building, gray amidst the wild greenery, and says to him for the first time, "That's where your father spent a year in prison." He will say no more.

First Year

In the time between darkness and daybreak, in the mourning
hours, the old dawn parts into plates of mosaic, blue and white
from the shadow black of the Slovak hillside.

They could never keep time, or slow it down together.

He counts the seconds before leaving the wedding bed
for the prison yard. Daily, in the sunswallowing afternoons,
it is hard labor. He counts the boulders breaking down the hours

until dusk lays its golden head behind the silent mountains.
Nightly, he bribes his guards' soft hearts with Moravian
wine, the touch of rabbit skins, the name of his new bride.

They let him pass through the moonsplintered gates
to sleep with her.

She waits for the dark to trace his face like fingers on fogged glass,
kiss each eye closed, and wash the day's dirt from his feet. The steam
from the kettle whistles on the stove, and she daydreams him now—

in smoke scent, his almond eyes and the creases in his lip lines.
He rubs her neck, fingers dripping across shoulders and down her back,
remembering the remembered and how, like steam, he will evaporate.

Darkness washes over the hills. He follows a path of starlight
bright enough for him to re-chart the areas he once was—
valley of the back, canyon of the neck. He could remember

everything of her—whether it has happened or not.

She would sing to him

Čierne oči choďte spať.

(Čierne oči choďte spať, bo musíte ráno vstať,
bo musíte ráno vstať.)

> Black eyes go to sleep.

> (Black eyes go to sleep, because you must awake
> in the morning,
> because you must awake in the morning.)

Ráno, ráno, ráničko.

(Ráno, ráno, ráničko, keď vychodí slniečko,
keď vychodí slniečko.)

> Morning, morning, early morning.

> (Morning, morning, morning, when the sun is rising,
> when the sun is rising.)

Cousin Cooper Writes from America

for hope that you will one day join us. If only the wind could lift you
or the land would bridge the water's back. We hear of the empty soil
you work daily. There is a land here you call your own. The future,
dreaming, grows green and tall enough to block the sky. There is a
copper woman the size of a mountain. She holds fire in her torch
leading you to shore. We have settled near the water of three rivers,
reflecting the light back to the sun. It shines brighter here and we
do not hunger. There is work and steel and money. You say there is
already a punishing wind coming in from the north. We know how
children's feet freeze bare in winter. Think of their curled toes and
how they'd warm by our fire. We send you our prayers in cloth and
money and words for hope of a voyage, a future you can give them.

III Voyage

After working in the fields till sundown, sifting

a few round tuber buds from the earth's barren belly,
he straightens up, looks out towards the range
and imagines water, the expanse of the sea,
and how it will carry them across.

Instructions for Immigrant Passengers

The Aquitania, July 26, 1929

1. Find a bucket, Mother—wash your three boys clean:
   dig dirt from Jon's fingernails, slick
   sweat back from Pavel's ears,
   scrub Andrej's elbows, knees

      (until they blush, raw as red potatoes).

2. Inspect hair for lice—be thorough:
   pick the skin cells along their scalps,
   brush their greased hair back from their eyes

      (tell them to always keep looking forward).

3. Unpack newly sewn cloth:
   pressed white cotton shorts,
   clean white collars,
   fresh white socks

      (dress them quickly, immaculate).

4. Follow to the loading dock:
   join the bodies pushing toward a border
   of land and water, a ship departing

      (continue, forward, together).

5. Officers will speak in English:
   chewing the words in their mouths,
   arms directing the traffic into two lines

      (avoid the separating, forward).

6. One officer will notice you—Father, speak your tongue:
   Moja rodina.
   Point to your family

   (rely on your hand's language, pointing forward).

7. Believe in all misunderstanding

   (the officer will choose volume, intimidation).

8. Do not move. Point:
   Moje deti.
   Point to your three silent children

   (they always keep looking forward).

9. Believe in losing communication

   (the officer will shake fists, his head, *no*—).

10. Do not move. Point:
    Moja žena.
    Point to your young wife

    (the officer's gaze will linger on her).

11. Believe in the persistence of belief:
    Ideme do Ameriky.
    Point to your names on a paper list

    (point and do not move, until he lets you

                                    forward).

Water

From the first night
     on deck
the weather   is hard
     wind and   rain rattling
eardrums   as they try
     to sleep.   A woman offers
them room   in her cabin.
     Once inside
the boys remember the womb,
curling themselves up, kissing their knees,
cradled between seat cushions and pillow,
     rocked within the ship's hull.

The warm walls of the cabin muffle
the dark water world, the night Atlantic,
the gull's call.

     Every morning, they are pulled from the
warmth of this den, reborn in the sun and spray, learn
how to walk again,
re-mastering the rhythm   of steps
     required   to cross
     the undulating
     floor   on water   to   land.

IV Rootings

They choose a plot on Goldstrohm Lane in Duquesne

next to a grove of fruit trees and a small stream to dam
up during the summer days.

Alcove

Brick upon stone, a growing
                    foundation,
he builds a new family home up
from the ground
                    cement and marble
tile to ceiling
beam and red oak
                    he paid for with cash.

As the children grow
                    in numbers
to thirteen, more boys
than girls, the rooms seem
                    smaller with time.

Upstairs, a bed of boys,
five bodies—toes to a nose,
                    an elbow
in a face—and in the winter,
a warmth they've earned from breath,

the youngest makes a bed
                    in the alcove,
its space, a darkness
lit by silence, by vowels
                    in a poem he whispers.

Premature

When the brick house on the corner
       emptied of her husband and boys
    double-shifting
      steel at the mill,
the Duquesne Police came
    and knocked on the front door.
       "Someone reported y'uns
for havin' a cow in your yard."

She answered in Slovak
      holding her spine
        to support her belly, like this,
   and pointed,
"Moja krava." [4]

The dairy cow was tied
    to the apple trunk bark
      in the back yard thicket
     double-shifting
       milk, butter, and cheese,
and when they shoved past her
    she ran behind,
      ballooning with weighty breath,
    water breaking beneath her.

She cried out,
    "Detská!
     Moje detská!" [5]
       two months too early
and the police delivered them both,
    stillborn,
      taking her past away.

Darning for the Infant

        It is a gift
how she_ needles_
       _the_thread_without _looking_._
_Basting_a_band_of_lace_to_sapphire_silk_,_
       _she_leads__the_silver_through_
_the_fabrics_by_thumb_and_forefinger_,_
       tugs _ _at_the_strand_and_ _ _pulls_
_the_point_up_ _ _toward_the_sky_,_
       _then_under_the_soft_lining_again_,_
_a_circular_motion_
       through _ _ _ _ _ _ _and_tug_._
_ When_the_overlocking_is_finished_and_the_needle   bare,
       all pins pulled out of place,

       she holds up the hollow oak body of the Infant of Prague,
       a clothed newborn reaching out to be held,
       and imagines how her stitchwork would have lain
       on warm bodies.

She continues, ties a new knot to her needle,
prays with her fingers,
       _prays_with_thread_._

...*Silent Night, Holy Night*

Andy / John / Paul / brothers work steel at the mill ... the cells divide / move on / conquer / spread ... Teresa / Mary / Anka / sisters share songs, dances, recipes ... throat / lungs / breast / stomach wrought ... *All is calm, all is bright* ... where iron ore is reduced / smelted ... warm pink inner walls ... coke and limestone in a blast furnace ... acid somersaults kicking out their flesh ... *Round yon Virgin Mother and Child* ... producing molten iron ... throat / lungs / breast / stomach ... cast into pig iron ... twisted tubular structures ... impurities of sulfur / excess carbon removed ... *Holy infant so tender and mild* ... topical anesthesia / endoscopy ... alloying manganese / nickel / chromium ... weight loss / fatigue / poor motion of gut ... producing the exact steel required ... radiation, chemotherapy ... molten iron ... pouring over ... their yellow eyes ...

Sleep in heavenly peace, sleep in heavenly peace.

The Monday Garbage Man

of Goldstrohm Lane

would yell to the boy in the alley

> *Hey!   Meester Jimmy!*
> *Yezush, Maryja, an Yozef!*
> *I vork   tventy year   and*
> *   steel   you   put*
> *hedda fish   in da can,*

and pointing into the foul tin can

> *moje nose vant   keel me,*
> *Chrystus!   Why for you*
> *no put   czekoladka,*
> *   no Pilsner,*
> *PespiKola   in   can?*

he'd threaten the neighborhood

> *Jus tink it.   Vat if*
> *   I strajku,   an no*
> *pick up,   huh?   Vat den?*

with vulgar pests, teaching the boy

> *If trash stay   bahneet*
> *   door front   house,*
> *an raccoony   come for*
> *food?   Dey make da shit!*

how to loosen dirt on his tongue.

> *You crazy   fish muddah!*
> *   Dis smell   like hell.*
> *Christ!*

V The Mills

There was a seed planted in a young boy's head.

One day in the kitchen, in front of his mother, it sprouted
and grew out of the boy's mouth. Seeing this, his older brother
grabbed him and shook the plant to its root, dislodging it.
The boy coughed it up, freeing the seedling to grow elsewhere.

In a Mill Town

The mid-afternoon clouds are pregnant with ash
and the red dust falls gently over Homestead,
Braddock, and Duquesne.

It flurries and settles along car tops, window shingles,
sticks to hair and inner lung walls with a rusty hue.

They walk home during lunch hour to wash the pigment
from their skin, wondering when winter comes
if the snow will be whiter than pink.

The Orchard

*"We were so poor,
someone forgot to tell us."*

The flatfoot farm boys climb
the twittle timber fruit trees
behind the billowing back bricks
and winter wicker willows.

The young Tom thumbs
the boughs like a drum.

Day-dreaming boys 'n berry blues
pick pear pits, apple core, plum petals,
finger licks of peach rind,
and spits of cherry sticks.

Playing the princes of pie,
they hoard heartful hands
of fruit into their shabby shorts,
pocket seams sag with savory smiles.

Lips are limbs of nectar that boys have sugared,
seeding sweet teeth till suppertime.

Big Bertha of the Steel Mills

Duquesne, PA

She is aging fast, a furnace, exhaling
heavy chrome smoke into the morning
air that hugs the icicles on twining
oaks, silver along the Monongahela.

She is their god of steel
mills where men work fierce as fire
ants, faces striped with soot
that seeps in, a permanent pigment.

They keep feeding her coals,
orange, sparking, thrashing,
working her liquids into iron red
instead of copper, zinc, or gold.

Carnegie once said he loved her first.
My father's father and brothers know
her best. They mold her fluids into the lean
skeletons of bridges and skyscrapers.

Long after their organs go black,
they will switch her blasting furnace off.
She will turn cold, scabbed and silent,
raveled in roots and blood-brown rust.

VI Sacrifice

After bringing him to see the rabbit coop

behind his mother's old house, he pointed to an Angora,
its long white hair unlike any other he'd seen, and said,
"Beautiful." That night when he asked what was in the stew,
they said, the one he had chosen.

Children's Song

Kohútik jarabý
> Spotted rooster

nechoď do záhrady
> you cannot go to the garden,

polámeš ľaliu
> you'll damage the lilies

potom ťa zabijú
> and later you'll be killed.

A keď ťa zabijú
> And when you've been killed

tak ťa pochovajú
> you'll be buried

do takej záhrady
> in that same garden

kde vtáčky spievajú
> where the birds are singing.

Prague Spring

Czechoslovakia, August 21, 1968

There was a night rumbling
as if the earth tossed in its sleep—

Red Stars pointing
gun barrels out of their chests—

tank tread along the cobbles of
Wenceslas Square—

and they were there: Hammers and Sickles—
in case thoughts themselves had sprung twelve toes—

ran the streets rampantfree and thinking!

There was a night rumbling
as if something stirred to waking—
and he was there: a Molotov cocktail—
a flag flyer until dawn—

and she was there: as silent as gesture—
stronger than language—a middle finger—

but Spring sister, my fallen rebel of the night!
they should have told you

that stars would shoot at your chest—
that a quiet could come from protest.

Exiled

"Rusové přišli." / "The Russians have come."

In the early morning his uncle woke him he said his uncle woke him saying to pack his bag his bag was a suitcase he said a suitcase of all the words that couldn't fit in his mouth only his suitcase and the clothes on his back American khaki he said a foreigner's cloth on his back he said the torch was in front he said the torch was attached to the buckboard the buckboard his uncle used in the fields he said the buckboard was led by one horse the one horse followed the dog he said followed over the hill over the hill to where the trains were he said to where the Russians had stopped all the trains stopped the trains and took him he said they took his bag he said took him to the train toilet and locked him inside he said they searched his bag searched his words he said and the train had traveled for hours he said they brought his bag back emptied of all his words he said brought it back empty except for a shirt hanging out like a tongue he said the train was filled with foreigners and no one knew why he said the train was soon full but the town signs were changed he said they stopped the train he said they unlocked the door they pushed him out he said pushed him out with their guns guns to his back they said they told him get on the bus they said get on the bus and he thought he could run he said he might have run but their guns he said and he thought he had more time there could be more time he said so he got on the bus all got on the bus all silent on the bus he said thinking it was their last thinking it was a cliff he said a cliff and a gunshot to the head Jesus Christ he said Jesus he'd forgotten forgotten how to pray he said and the bus had stopped the bus stopped and they were forced he said forced out and unloaded across the border they crossed into Vienna he said and no one knew why

Torch No. 1

"One must fight against the kind of evil that he is able to defeat." —Jan Palach, January 19, 1969

At four   o'clock,
          beneath
the pigeon stone shadow
          of Wenceslas Square,
                    kindling
          more flame than the

                              firefly

          pinned
to the felt of Natural History,

a boy
          fell
                    a human
                              torch
                    by the side
          of the road

and they would not treat the body—
how easily doctors
          follow   orders.

Smell the cooked flesh,
                    how it lingers,
                              skin,
                                        like cinders
                    on the air,
                    sheets,
ashy with body marks—

See how simply
            the cells
                        blister   apart,
thin tissue dissolving,
                        pink   ravines carved
            into hardened black.

Lick the dried crust of gasoline
                                    clean
            from your ears
                        and hear the
                                    burning.

VII The Village

We take the train from Prague to Humenné as a family

and follow the tradition: piling ham and salami, cheese, tomato,
cucumber, butter on a fresh baguette. Cut it one, two, three,
for breakfast, lunch, and dinner. Toast a glass of red
wine, the way his father taught him
on the trains he calls libraries.

Below the Tatra Mountains

Before the August sun
and white hay are rolled
along the flats of green wilder,
the thorn grass is still high
enough for me to get down
deep into it.

I would want to be a locust,
to taste the dandelions,
their green wings soft
as the wool on herds that feed
along the brook, its blue running
through the blades I lie on.

I would want to brush my legs
against their stems to hear
what melody the green can play
for the bronzed wheat and sun-
flowers boughing up their necks
to the threshed sky.

And when the clouds collide,
romancing each other until the rain
bathes the mountains, I would raise
my wings to smell the pine green
of the forest where the doe
hides among the aspen.

And if I could climb
to the crest of a corn stalk,
I would want to see the change
of hues on the patched earth,
a world in its wealth
of green.

Circle Game

Dressed in matching floral prints, my mother leads us to the middle
of the room and adds us to the circle of young girls holding hands.

They smile and nod as I grab my sister's palm and our cousin's
while she begins to lead the ring around.

This is the direction of the circle game,
it moves like a clock around the wooden floor.

We hold onto each other, fingers fastened like braided hair,
and we follow, repeating in rhythm with foreign words.

I do not know the wheel of the mill we sing: *Kolo, kolo mlynské...*
nor the value of four old coins... *za štyri rýnske...*

All I know is the way our tongues roll against the tops of our mouths—
we are full of O, and consonants that stick our feet to the ground.

We sing: *kolo sa nám polámalo...* not knowing the wheel has broken
a do vody popadalo... and landed in the water below.

I run laugh run my short legs round faster,
as our hips swooshswing our dresses full of summer...

And splash! *Urobilo bác!* Just as fast,
we stop the clock, let go, and all fall to the floor.

They teach us the way back up again, staying low at first,
hunched at our chubknees and miming a motion with our forearms

Vezmeme si hoblík, pílku... as if it were a saw we've taken up
zahráme sa ešte chvíľku... to rebuild the wheel in moments.

I imagine it a violin on the air, mimicking the music in our mouths,
rising taller as I play the sounds of this language filling our ears.

And when we finish, *až to kolo spravíme...* fully grown, we smile,
táááák sa zatočíme!... knowing how the length of a vowel

gives us time to turn around—and spin the colors
of our dresses, flower petals across the floor.

Kneading

I watch my great aunt flour the wooden table. She says the round of the bowl gives form to the salt, yolk, and onions her hands knead from memory. I roll my sleeves and stab a finger through the dough, rising as if it wanted breath, then press it down to the wood with my palm. She hands me the rolling pin. I push it to the white mound, down–forward, back–down–forward—and again—feeling the burn root in my upper arm. She knows this is not my talent. She pretends to roll it out in the air beside me, showing how to push faster, stronger, a woman. I know this is not my talent. I show her I can pinch the dough thin—into squares, that roundness cannot hold the swelling at the center where the tin boils.

She takes the pin, rolls the dough flat in seconds—
the motion, a recipe aged to taste.

She fills some with potato, some with jam—
some with memory she is always kneading.

Summer Pick

This afternoon in Prague,
        the tourists   invade
                the walkspace.
The air is street   dust   and sweat
and we crave a cooling down—
        a scoop or two of *Stracitella*
                in a cone.

The corner vendor is free
        and Father   steps up   with the money.
                A crowd emerges   around him,
                    ants to the sugar.
                        He feels them
                        on his back,
                checking the flavors,
                noticing his children
                and where his money   comes from.

They call us
        "beautiful girls"
and he thanks them   while he turns to our mother,
                    passing the treats
                    back.
                The cream dripping
                        to hot cement,
we think only the sweet
anticipation,
        letting *be be finale of seem*,
the intoxication—
        The only emperor is the emperor
                of ice-cream.

And the exchange is done.
Walking away
he feels
light,
a fullness of forget,
hands pat
his shirt pockets,
and finds his wallet has left
with the crowd.

VIII Reading the Ground

After lying in the sun and tall grass of the island I can hear

the sound as it moves in fast, spreading out in the heat
on the sky. It grows louder as it travels, now taking out the sun.
In this shaded darkness, there is a moment when I am one
with the electricity in the air and in the ground.
My skin, my eyes, my island—electric.

Sunday Picnic on the Vltava

Střelecký ostrov, Prague

The waves of air along the water
soothe the chapped spines of young
Czechs who've sheared their hair
to hawk it up and away from sweat
that pearls along their skull lines.

They gather clinking Pilsner bottles,
punk among the mosquito weeds and silted
rock the flood has left on the island strip.
They know the embankment well,
each grass stain and joint

drag, another hip conversation
raveled with the island boles.
Their black Levis, tied with ropes,
are cut at the knees and dragged down
to moon the Jazz boats and ducks they feed

with hard baguettes. And where they lose
their footing in the muddy underledge
of the river, they meet their reflections
in water. Wet-handling their girls,
they pull them down deeper

into darkness until body parts obscure,
the only light reflecting like cracked beer
bottle bits along the ripples the paddleboats
leave behind. One emerges wearing
his girl's swim top—leaving her

on display—to ask if it looks good
on his broader shape. Beside him, a boy
scraping up earth to build mud mounds,
protecting the bank from swans,
looks on and learns how to be a man.

The Painter on the Charles Bridge

We thought he was a sweat stain upon the rim
stones that bridge across Charles Bridge, his leathered
skin as red as the eyes of pigeons that burrow
among the bread crumbs on his cobbled mattress.

He sat shirtless, pressing his backbone against
the cool granite. Pushing a pair of plastic horns
back into his greased curls, he'd hiss at reflections
passing across the window glass of jewelry shops.

We thought his mind had rusted and stalled.
But, mistaking his eyes for garnets behind the panes,
he saw himself as Kolar or Picasso, inking newspaper
canvas with his fingerprints, self-portraits of Satan.

Gathering his demons up for sale, he would lick
at our ankles, spit at our sins until the sunlight turned to fire
above *Hradčany* Castle. When his eyes went black at night,
the rock beneath him crumbled. He knew to pack away his horns.

We did not know which stair he took to exile himself,
if he tossed his many faces into the falls, baptized by the Vltava,
or if he prostrated all night beneath the bronze crucifix,
or kissed the stone toes of King Charles at the bridge's end.

Even now, as we walk along the pebbled palms of the broken
brickwork, leading us toward the gates of Malá Strana,
we think it odd how the pigeons gather with eyes of rubies,
pecking at a shadow left upon the stone.

The *Kostnice* in Kutná Hora

*"It's estimated that the chapel now contains
the bones of up to 40,000 people."*

I.

At first, the stones could not fit
all the names, and then the ground
could no longer hold, so they were piled
outside along the stone walling—bodies
as slabs alongside walkways growing
in number as if watered among the spurge
root and moss between the Church stone—a cheek
pressed to a cold abdomen—the body listened
longingly for a heartbeat or the warmth of a chest
rising with air.

2.

The pathways became tunnels of limbs
upon limbs, and the children
asked if they remembered all of their names,
and the priest gathered up what was left,
choosing the largest bones,
separating people into pieces.

3.

The monk's blind eyes could feel the strength of a femur, the flat curvature
of a clavicle to rest a chin upon. Holding the nasal cavity, he'd polish
the frontal lobe and inspect the skull's orbits; ensuring the eyes were
equidistant and uniform, he'd place one beneath the other in geometrical
lines cascading down the wall on both sides of a large chalice of legs and
arms. His fingers worked the fibula and humerus into proper position,
building a new body of bones for the blood of Christ.

4.

I had imagined walking into a cellar built of bone walls with no light,
an underground crypt where my flesh was removed upon entering,
and I agreed among these naked rows of remains to shed this weight
in the stripping down to the bones that built me—

5.

As I wait my turn I watch
children pose, giggling in front
of the Schwarzenberg crest,
the bone bird pecking the eye
from a skull, a raven attacking
an invading soldier.

> *The living frighten me here.*
> *I will not smile*
> *in front of this many dead.*

6.

It is considered a treasure,
this chandelier of fingers and toes.
It hangs, pointing down from the center
of the chapel's noughts-and-crosses floorplan.
I point back,
notice how the phalanges are threaded, spread out
so that no matter which way we walk
within the crosspath,
the dead can always reach us.

7.

I imagine my ancestral bones here. Her hands chosen for the
altarpiece—a palm to cradle the infant statue, his strong shoulders
to support the base of the cross. After bearing thirteen new bodies
into this world, their pelvic bones would adorn the shrine to the Holy
Family, for others to pray for their bones' bones to outlive them.

8.

The stone inside is colder
than soil in the sun.

    Listen.

You can hear them.
Vespers on the dusty air.

> *Bury me with you*
> *in the fields outside*
> *so the spuds can bloom*
> *in the curvature of my eye.*

Reading the Ground

We ask how far as they point toward the crucifix at the top of the hill and we continue to hike along the indentations of hardened mud left by the tractor wheels. They point out the potato fields, the grazing land, the silent volcano. My brother strays off the path, thrashing through the tall grass in his Levi brown cords, pulling at the long weeds and whacking a walkway in his youth. My sister keeps to the middle, stop and go, picking bundles of wildflowers, tying daisy chains to her long hair and wishing on dandelions. I follow behind, reading the ground, avoiding the cow pies and pockets of tadpole water from the summer rain. I stop and turn to see the distance we've come, noticing the way the land colors shift in the sunlight, a patchwork of earth in three directions and continuous horizon. When I turn back, I can just make them out at the top of the hillside like sunflowers swaying in the wind. I keep filling in the footsteps walked before me until I reach the top where they've gathered, stones around the foot of the cross.

VIV Slovak Lessons in the Language

[1] *Czar·das*   [chahr-dahsh]

—noun

1. a Slavic and Hungarian folk-dance of alternating slow (*lassu*) and fast sections (*friss*):

> I watch my cousins dance a **czardas**—
> they carry themselves proudly and improvise,
> their snapping feet, inward and outward,
> the couples whirling in unison to

2. a piece of music composed for or in the rhythm of this dance:

> The Gypsy orchestra play a **czardas** in 2/4 time,
> a courting compelling them
> in syncopated rhythms.

(2) *Sliv·o·vitz* [sliv-uh-vits]

—noun

1. a dry, usually colorless, slightly bitter plum brandy
   from Eastern Europe:

> When my stomach pang worsened to stabbing
> daggers, and I lay face down in bed, our cousins
> would tell my mother to mix a shot of **slivovitz**
> into my Cola—village medicine.

(3) *O·ko* [o-ko]

—*noun*, plural *oči* [oh-chee]

1. the organ of sight, in vertebrates typically one
   of a pair of spherical bodies
   contained in an orbit of the skull:

   > Years after, she cries to her son, revealing
   > the secret, how her brother Stephan died
   > at her feet, stabbed in the *oko* with an ice pick
   > by a jealous wedding guest. When the murderer
   > was later found blinded by thorns, the police came
   > to arrest her new husband, charged
   > with the maiming, and put him in prison
   > for the first year of their marriage.

2. this organ with respect to the color of the iris:

   > They said that her *oči* matched the color
   > of distant waters, perhaps found farther
   > than the Tatras or Vltava, a deeper blue
   > than the three rivers. It is the blue of another
   > world, time, or love.

(4) *Kra·va* [klah-vah]

—*noun*, plural **kravy**

1. the mature female of a bovine animal, especially of the
    genus *Bos*:

> After sun down, the heifers leave
> the herd, bellies full. They chew the cud
> between their flat-topped teeth,
> their barrels of bodies bound homeward
> on a slow return from the fields,
> a day's graze in the Humenné hills.
>
> Down the pathways of dirt road
> and past the stucco walls of village homes,
> I can hear the ringing of copper bells
> around their thick necks as they pass.
>
> Each **krava** breaks off from the line
> of freckled hides, knowing her own way
> home. Ours turns up the drive, walks
> her tired hooves into the wooden stall
> behind the house, and waits for us
> to gate her in.

(5) *Det·ská* [det-ska]

—noun, plural ***deti***

1. an infant or very young child:

> He was so young, but can remember his sister Helen,
> a ***detská*** of five months, and how beautiful
> she looked—her pixie lashes and opal skin,
> so still as if she were dreaming.

—adjective, ***detskej***

2. of or suitable for a baby:

> He still remembers how they buried
> that ***detskej*** coffin.

(6) *Slnko* [slun-koh]

—*noun*

1. the star that is the central body of the solar system,
    around which the planets revolve and from which they
    receive light and heat:

> On Sunday, as children, we would sleep
> until the ***slnko*** snuck through the window, a pest
> tracing our cheeks. We would sing together,
> awake with language:

> "When the *mesiac* (moon) and the *hviezdy* (stars)
> come together in the sky, then the ***slnko*** waits till
> morning just to hit you in the eye."

ABOUT THE AUTHOR

Tera Vale Ragan received her BA in Creative Writing from The University of Southern California where she received the Virginia Middleton Award and the Undergraduate Creative Writing Award for poetry. Tera recently received her MFA at San Francisco State where she was a poetry editor of *Fourteen Hills* and winner of the Mark Linenthal Award. She is currently a poetry editor for *Rattapallax Magazine.* Her poems have appeared in journals including *Rattle, Transfer, Eclipse, Hot Metal Bridge, Barely South Review, 16th & Mission Review,* and *Ekleksographia.* She spends her summers writing in Prague, Czech Republic.

ABOUT THE ARTIST

Lorna Alkana's artwork uses layers of lines, colors, and language to create visual essays for a digital world. Lorna graduated from USC and is a Teach for America alum. She is the artist of a graphic biography of the French feminist Suzanne Voilquin's *A Solitary Path*, published by The Graphic History Project. Some of her other publications include *A Surreal Coloring and Story Book* and *Windows: A Story Told Through Windows, Frames and Screens.* She discusses and animates her blog (lornaalkana.com) where she lives in Los Angeles, California.

ABOUT THE WORD WORKS

The Word Works, a nonprofit literary organization, publishes contemporary poetry and presents public programs.

The Hilary Tham Capital Collection presents work by poets who volunteer for literary nonprofit organizations. Nominations are due from qualifying 501(c)3 nonprofits by April 1, manuscript submissions by May 1. Other imprints include International Editions, the Washington Prize (book publication and a monetary award for an American or Canadian poet), and, starting in 2014, The Tenth Gate.

Monthly, The Word Works offers free literary programs in the Chevy Chase, MD, Café Muse series, and each summer, it holds free poetry programs in Washington, DC's Rock Creek Park. Annually in June, two high school students debut in the Joaquin Miller Poetry Series as winners of the Jacklyn Potter Young Poets Competition. Since 1974, Word Works programs have included: "In the Shadow of the Capitol," a symposium and archival project on the African American intellectual community in segregated Washington, DC; the Gunston Arts Center Poetry Series (featuring Ai, Carolyn Forché, and Stanley Kunitz); the Poet Editor panel discussions at The Writer's Center (including John Hollander, Maurice English, Anthony Hecht, Josephine Jacobsen); and Master Class workshops (with Agha Shahid Ali, Thomas Lux, Marilyn Nelson).

As a 501(c)3 organization, The Word Works has received awards from the National Endowment for the Arts, the National Endowment for the Humanities, the DC Commission on the Arts & Humanities, the Witter Bynner Foundation, Poets & Writers, The Writer's Center, Bell Atlantic, the David G. Taft Foundation, and others, including many generous private patrons. The Word Works has established an archive of artistic and administrative materials in the Washington Writing archive housed in the George Washington University Gelman Library. The Word Works is a member of the Council of Literary Magazines and Presses and distributed by Small Press Distribution.

More information at WordWorksBooks.org.

TO OUR SUPPORTERS

We wish to thank the generous donors whose contributions to the Hilary Tham Capital Collection made this year's books possible. In addition to some who asked to remain anonymous, we also extend gratitude to Karren Alenier, Nathalie Anderson, James Beall, Sandra Beasley, Mel Belin, Doris Brody, W. Perry Epes, Barbara Goldberg, Joseph Goldberg, Stephen Hubbard, Tod Ibrahim, Brandon Johnson, Steven Klimah, Richard Lyons, Kathleen McCoy, Susan Laughter Meyers, Miles Moore, Debora Ragan, James Ragan, John E. Ragan, J. Courtney Reid, Brad Richard, Maritza Rivera, Hannah M. Stevens, Barbara Louise Ungar, Maria van Beuren, Mike White, Nancy White, Rosemary Winslow, Pamela Murray Winters, Michele Wolf, and Dallas Woodburn.

FROM THE HILARY THAM CAPITAL COLLECTION

Mel Belin, *Flesh That Was Chrysalis*
Doris Brody, *Judging the Distance*
Sarah Browning, *Whiskey in the Garden of Eden*
Grace Cavalieri, *Pinecrest Rest Home*
Christopher Conlon, *Gilbert and Garbo in Love* &
       Mary Falls: Requiem for Mrs. Surratt
Donna Denizé, *Broken like Job*
W. Perry Epes, *Nothing Happened*
Bernadette Geyer, *The Scabbard of Her Throat*
Barbara G. S. Hagerty, *Twinzilla*
James Hopkins, *Eight Pale Women*
Brandon Johnson, *Love's Skin*
Marilyn McCabe, *Perpetual Motion*
Judith McCombs, *The Habit of Fire*
Miles David Moore, *The Bears of Paris* & *Rollercoaster*
Kathi Morrison-Taylor, *By the Nest*
Maria Terrone, *The Bodies We Were Loaned*
Hilary Tham, *Bad Names for Women* & *Counting*
Barbara Louise Ungar, *Charlotte Brontë, You Ruined My Life*
Jonathan Vaile, *Blue Cowboy*
Rosemary Winslow, *Green Bodies*
Michele Wolf, *Immersion*

Other Available Word Works Books

ADDITIONAL TITLES

Karren L. Alenier, *Wandering on the Outside*
Karren L. Alenier, Hilary Tham, Miles David Moore, eds.,
      Winners: A Retrospective of the Washington Prize
Christopher Bursk, ed., *Cool Fire*
Barbara Goldberg, *Berta Broadfoot and Pepin the Short*
Jacklyn Potter, Dwaine Rieves, Gary Stein, eds.,
      Cabin Fever: Poets at Joaquin Miller's Cabin
Robert Sargent, *Aspects of a Southern Story* &
      A Woman From Memphis

CPSIA information can be obtained at www.ICGtesting.com
Printed in the USA
BVOW05s0533180814

362836BV00001B/15/P